D0416777

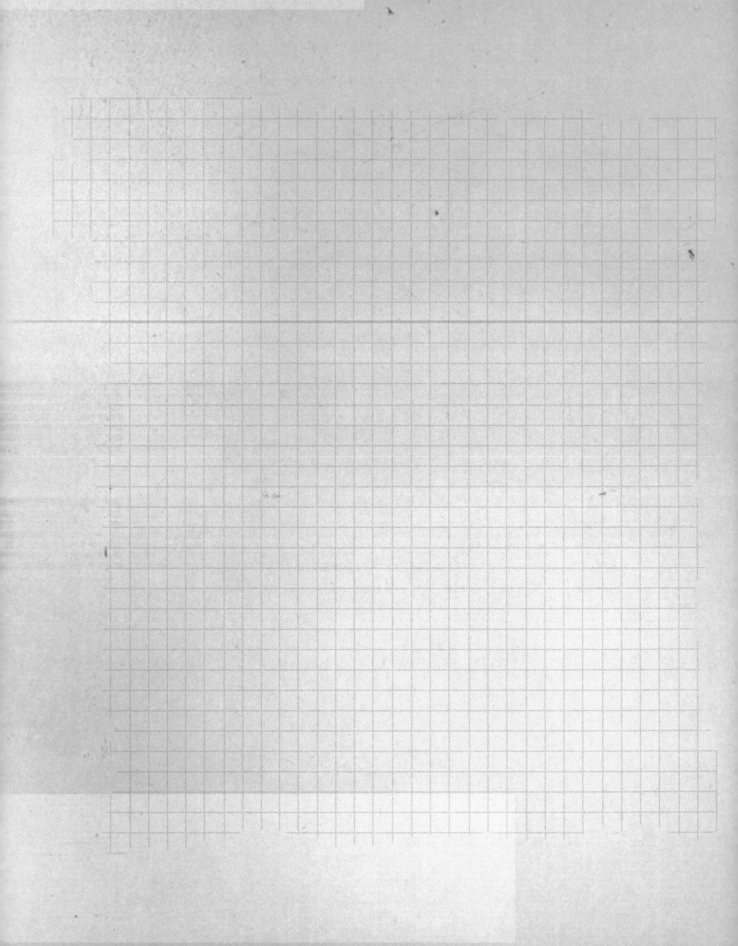

HOW TO DESIGN
THE WORLD'S BEST

SPORTS STADIUM

IN 10 SIMPLE STEPS

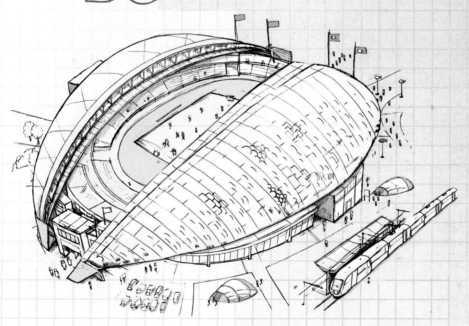

PAUL MASON

WAYLAND
www.waylandbooks.co.uk

First published in Great Britain in 2017 by Wayland

Copyright © Hodder and Stoughton Limited, 2017

Editor: Nicola Edwards
Design: Kevin Knight

Artwork by Tim Hutchinson

ISBN: 978 0 7502 9953 4
10 9 8 7 6 5 4 3 2 1

Wayland, an imprint of
Hachette Children's Group
Part of Hodder and Stoughton
Carmelite House
50 Victoria Embankment
London EC4Y 0DZ

An Hachette UK Company
www.hachette.co.uk
www.hachettechildrens.co.uk

Printed and bound in China

Picture acknowledgements:
All images courtesy of Shutterstock except
p11t, p14b and p26t Wikimedia Commons and p25 Alamy.

Every attempt has been made to clear copyright.
Should there be any inadvertent omission,
please apply to the publisher for rectification.

CONTENTS

Designing the world's best sports stadium   4

What makes the ideal sports stadium?   6

Step 1: draw a dream design   8

Step 2: make the stadium shimmer like a fish   10

Step 3: make sure the roof works   12

Step 4: check the playing surface   14

Step 5: moving people to and from the stadium   16

Step 6: get the shoppers underground!   18

Step 7: provide food and drink   20

Step 8: seating for everyone   22

Step 9: provide the stadium with power   24

Step 10: design a team kit   26

The best ever sports stadium?   28

Other top sports stadiums   30

'Work it out' answers   31

Glossary   32

Index   32

DESIGNING THE WORLD'S BEST SPORTS STADIUM

Imagine being at the Olympics and seeing one of your heroes win gold. Or seeing a championship-winning goal, or the first time a gymnastics move is done. Watching them on TV would be great – but it does not really show you the skill, speed and technique of the athletes. To see that, you actually have to be there.

Seeing sport live is way more exciting than watching it on TV – especially if your team wins!

Of course, watching live sport is not all good. It sometimes takes ages to get to the stadium. The seats for spectators are often uncomfortable and a bit too tightly packed. (At least being squished up against your neighbours keeps you warm on cold days!) Sometimes it's not easy to see what's happening on the pitch. It can take ages to get food, drink, or visit the toilet – and missing the crucial score because you are waiting in a queue is really annoying.

Imagine designing a dream sports stadium. It wouldn't have any of those problems – and it might just have some features no one has ever thought of before. In fact, it MIGHT just be the best sports stadium in the world.

How would you begin?

RESEARCH

Start by doing some research into top sports stadiums:

1) Ask your friends and family which stadiums they think are great and why.

2) Research famous stadiums in books, magazines and on the Internet.

Use your research to make a list of what makes a top stadium. It might include things like, 'Looks amazing' or 'easy to get to', for example. Use this list to make a survey, asking people what they think is most important in a sports stadium. There is an example of a survey like this on page 7.

Research Note

The best Internet researchers search using different combinations of words, for example:

world's best sports stadium

famous + sports + stadium

'design a sports stadium'

They also use more than one search engine (for example Google, DuckDuckGo and yippy.com). Use one of the search terms above in Google and DuckDuckGo to see why this is a good idea. Are the results the same, or different?

Architect Zaha Hadid designed the roof of the London Aquatics Centre to look like a giant wave. The centre hosted the swimming and diving competitions at the 2012 Olympic Games.

The Beijing National Stadium was built for the 2008 Olympics. Its unusual structure has led to it being nicknamed 'the Bird's Nest'.

WHAT MAKES THE IDEAL SPORTS STADIUM?

One good way for a designer to find out what makes a great sports stadium is... ask people who visit stadiums! You can do this through a user survey. On the next page there is an example of a user survey. It might also give you some ideas for your own design.

THE DESIGN BRIEF

The stadium in this book is going to have 40,000 seats. It is for Northport Athletic, a football team that has just been bought by telecomms billionaire Tracey Clacker. She has been a fan of Northport Athletic since she was a kid. The stadium will be built beside some old, closed-down docks. Tracey wants the stadium to become an important part of the city of Northport. Other sports will be played there, and there will also be a shopping mall.

Finding space for a new stadium near a city centre is never easy. Old docklands often provide a good place to build.

Research Note

The questions for a user survey are suggested by your research.

For example, research might show that some sports stadiums are open to the weather, while others are indoor. So one question could be, "Do you prefer indoor or outdoor stadiums?"

NEW STADIUM HERE

SURVEY FACTS

SURVEY NUMBER: 1,000

SOURCE: social media, including followers of Wembley Stadium, Yankee Stadium and Maracana Stadium

LOCATIONS: Various, including London, UK; New York, USA; Rio de Janeiro, Brazil

AGES: 14+

1 How old are you?
a) 17 or under   92
b) 18–45   431
c) 45–65   358
d) 66 or over   119

2 Do you use a wheelchair to get around?
a) Yes   32
b) No   968

3 How do you get to the stadium?
a) Drive   603
b) Catch a train/bus   302
c) Walk/cycle   95

4 If you answered a) to question 3), would you use public transport to get to the stadium:
a) If it was possible?   87
b) If it was possible and quick?   203
c) If it was possible, quick and cheap?   313

5 How important is it for a stadium to look impressive from the outside?
a) Very important   788
b) Quite important   197
c) Not important   15

6 Which of these statements do you agree with most?
a) Seats that are sheltered from bad weather are important   540
b) Being out in bad weather is all part of the fun   387
c) Inside and outside are equally good   73

7 How important are the following to your enjoyment? (You can choose more than one answer.)
a) Tasty food and drink inside the stadium   833
b) Facilities such as toilets   698
c) Being able to get really close to the players   620
d) Speed of arrival and leaving the stadium   720
e) Comfortable, wide, padded seats   801
f) A view of the whole pitch   1000

All stadiums must provide a place where wheelchair users can watch the action.

If it rains, only half of this crowd will stay dry!

After all that research, plus the user survey, any designer would be full of ideas! Now it is time to start sketching out a dream design. This is a chance to draw the best sports stadium imaginable. (It might not turn out to be the final stadium – every bit of the design will have to be double-checked before it is included.)

One problem for sports stadiums is that they are often empty. This stadium is going to be different. A variety of sports will be played here, not only football. Visitors will also come when no sport is being played, because there are other attractions. There will be cafés and restaurants, a shopping mall and a sports centre.

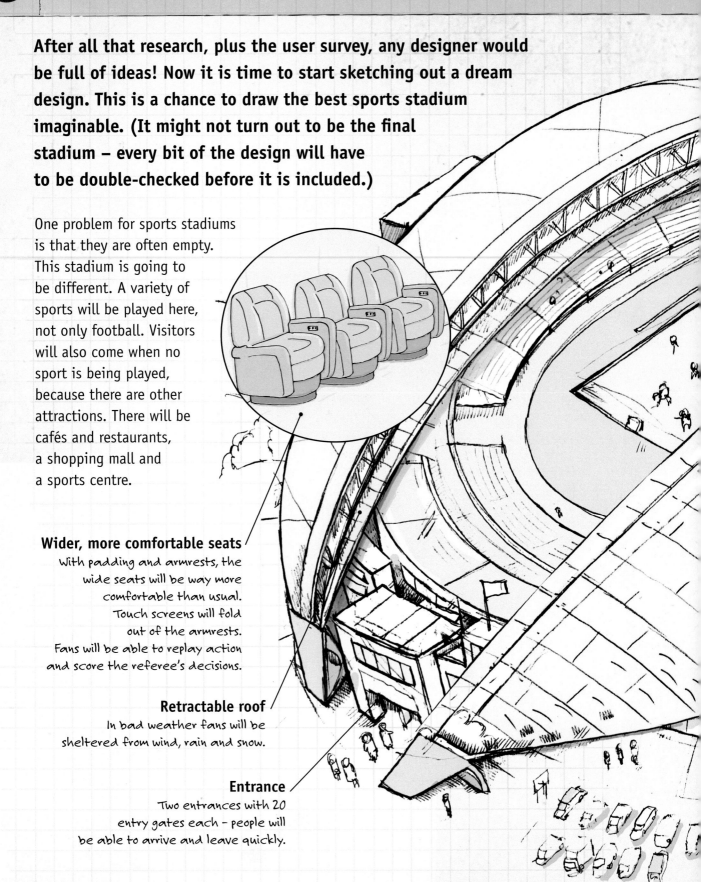

Wider, more comfortable seats
With padding and armrests, the wide seats will be way more comfortable than usual. Touch screens will fold out of the armrests. Fans will be able to replay action and score the referee's decisions.

Retractable roof
In bad weather fans will be sheltered from wind, rain and snow.

Entrance
Two entrances with 20 entry gates each – people will be able to arrive and leave quickly.

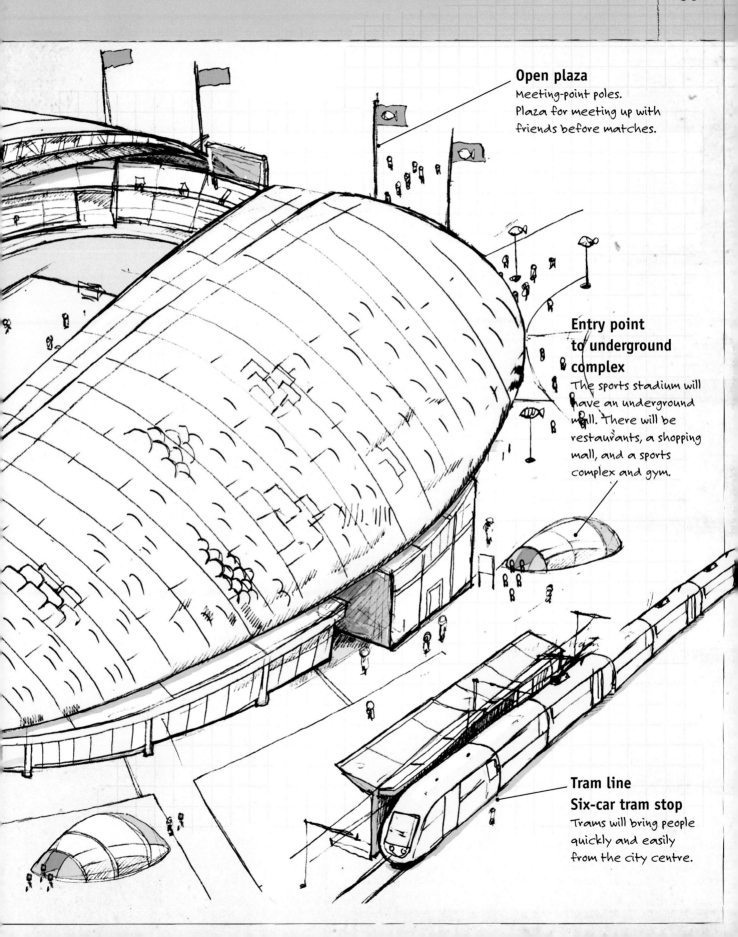

Open plaza
Meeting-point poles.
Plaza for meeting up with
friends before matches.

**Entry point
to underground
complex**
The sports stadium will
have an underground
mall. There will be
restaurants, a shopping
mall, and a sports
complex and gym.

**Tram line
Six-car tram stop**
Trams will bring people
quickly and easily
from the city centre.

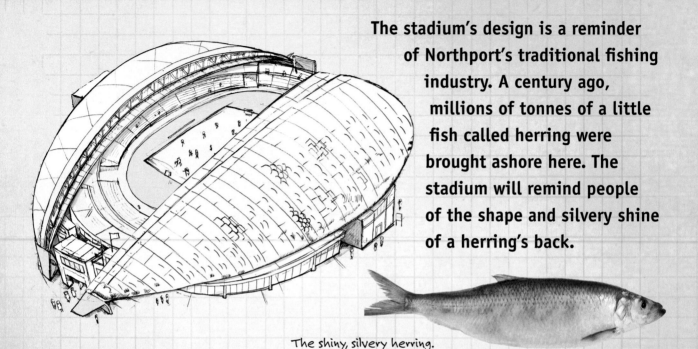

The stadium's design is a reminder of Northport's traditional fishing industry. A century ago, millions of tonnes of a little fish called herring were brought ashore here. The stadium will remind people of the shape and silvery shine of a herring's back.

The shiny, silvery herring.

Research Note

The herring is sometimes called 'the silver of the sea'. It got this name for two things: its silvery colour and its value. Herring is so valuable that in the 1500s, the Netherlands built a whole navy to defend its herring fishing boats. Herring is still valuable (and the cause of international disagreements) today.

WORK IT OUT!

Billionaire Tracey Clacker is willing to spend a LOT of money on the stadium. She has set a budget of £350 million. The budget is made up of three main parts:

55% to build the stadium
35% to build the shopping mall
10% on the plaza, roads, tram stops and lines, etc

How much money is available for each part? (You can check your answers on page 31.)

DESIGN CHALLENGES

In the user survey, 788 out of 1000 people said the stadium's appearance is really important. This throws up a design challenge. For the sides to look like a herring's back they should be silvery, like herring scales. You will need to find out whether this is possible.

WORK IT OUT!

Is it possible to make a building's outside look like shiny, silvery fish skin?

Start by doing an Internet image search for:
- shiny + building
- silvery + building
- fish skin building

You could also go to a public library to find out about an architect called Frank Gehry. Gehry is famous for being inspired by the fish his mum used to keep in the bath!

THE FINAL DESIGN

In the final design, the stadium is going to be covered in metallic tiles, like one of Frank Gehry's famous buildings. These will be arranged to look like fish scales.

WORK IT OUT!

How many panels will be needed to cover the sides of the stadium?

Each side will be 276m long and have an area of 30,788m². Each tile is rectangular and 1m long x 1m high. The tiles will need to overlap by 0.1m on two sides.

To work out the area, first work out the exposed area of each tile. Then divide this into the area of one of the stadium's sides. Finally double your number, since the stadium has two sides.

Check your answer on page 31.

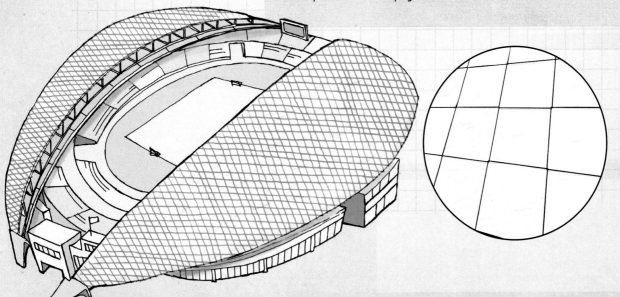

MAKE SURE THE ROOF WORKS

In the dream design, the stadium has a retractable roof. This will slide across and provide shelter when the weather is bad. Most of the time, though, the roof will be open and matches will be held outdoors. The roof is expensive, so first you have to decide whether it is a good idea.

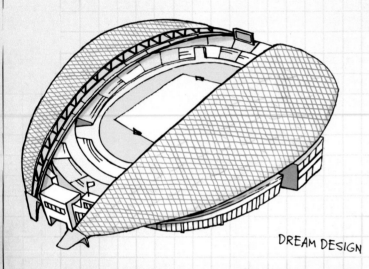

DREAM DESIGN

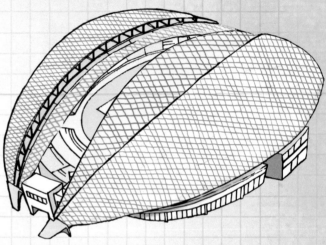

WORK IT OUT!

Look back at the user survey on page 7. Use the results to work out what percentage of people thought sheltered seats were important in a top stadium.

To do this, divide the number of people by the total number taking part in the survey. Then multiply this number by 100.

Check your answer on page 31.

RESEARCHING THE LOCAL CLIMATE

The user survey shows that most people want to be sheltered from bad weather – but will there actually be any bad weather? Next you need to research the local climate.

Research Note

The stadium is in the north and near the sea. This area experiences many kinds of weather:

Month:	Average temp. (°C):	Average rainfall (mm):	Average sunshine (hrs):	Average wind speed (kph):
December	5	61	3	15
March	5	49	6	13
June	12	51	9	15
September	12	47	6	15

Wind, rain, sunshine and even snow are all likely at some time during the year.

PICKING A ROOF

The local weather does mean a roof would be a good idea. There are two main types of retractable roof to choose from:
1) Roofs that turn the stadium into an indoor, climate-controlled space.
2) Roofs that simply provide shelter.
In the survey, most fans wanted to be sheltered. But lots of fans also liked being out in the air. A 'shelter' roof would work well for both groups.

The retractable roof over Wimbledon's Centre Court allows a tennis match to continue even in the rain.

WORK IT OUT!

Use the research note to work out whether a solid roof or a flexible one would be best. (Hint: the key question is whether the roof can be opened and closed in typical local weather.)

You can check your thinking on page 31.

Research Note

National Stadium, Warsaw

The retractable fabric roof can only be opened or closed if there is little wind, the temperature is above 5ºC and it is not raining.

Safeco Field, Seattle

Safeco Field's solid roof acts like an umbrella, giving shelter but also letting in outside air.

THE FINAL DESIGN

The final design is for a solid retractable roof, like the one in the dream design. A lightweight fabric roof would have been less expensive – but the local weather means it is not the best design.

Hidden guttering takes away rainwater
Rainwater used in stadium's toilets

Larger gap allows air to get inside the stadium

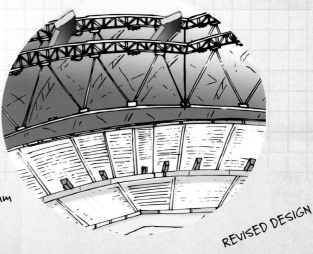

REVISED DESIGN

CHECK THE PLAYING SURFACE

In the original design, the stadium has a grass playing surface. The playing surface is going to be used for several sports. In just one week there might be hockey on Wednesday, rugby on Saturday and football on Sunday.

All the different sports will mean the stadium is always busy. Lots of people will visit, and it will be an important meeting-place for the city. This is just what Tracey Clacker wants. It does cause a problem for the designer, though.

DESIGN CHALLENGES

Some of the games being played will damage the pitch. After a rugby match on Saturday, for example, the playing surface will be all chewed up. In most stadiums, the pitch would have a week to recover. Here, though, there could be a football match the next day. You have to find a way to save the playing surface. Maybe your research can help?

Would you fancy playing on this pitch tomorrow? Nor would Northport Athletic's top footballers!

Research Note

The GelreDome Stadium (Arnhem, Netherlands)
Europe's first football stadium with a retractable pitch opened in 1996. The pitch is rolled out of the way for concerts, leaving a hard floor beneath.

University of Phoenix Stadium (Arizona, USA)
The grass playing surface is in a giant tray. It is mostly kept outside, in the sunshine. For matches, the tray is brought in on rail tracks.

Sapporo Dome (Sapporo, Japan)
The Sapporo Dome has TWO playing surfaces. Baseball matches are played on artificial turf. Then, when there is a football match on, seats are moved out of the way and a grass pitch is brought in from outside. It floats in on a bed of air, a bit like a hovercraft. (This is worth watching on the Internet!)

Sapporo Dome

GET THE SHOPPERS UNDERGROUND!

As well as lots of sports events, the stadium is going to have other attractions. There will be a gym and a swimming pool at the stadium. Under the surface of the plaza there is going to be a shopping mall. Tracey Clacker is going to lease the space to a company that already runs several big malls. The money will help pay for the stadium.

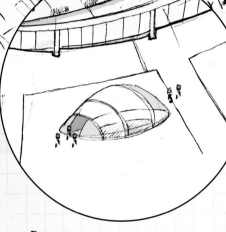

Entrance to mall from plaza

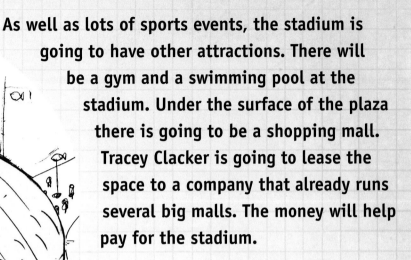

DESIGN CHALLENGES

The mall itself is being designed by an expert mall designer, so you do not have to worry about that. But the shoppers will be using escalators that lead down from the plaza. It is your job to make sure these can carry enough people. Otherwise, the plaza will get jammed up with shoppers.

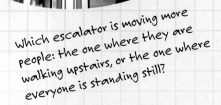

Which escalator is moving more people: the one where they are walking upstairs, or the one where everyone is standing still?

WORK IT OUT!

How many trams will be needed?

39,000 people will be arriving by tram. According to research, 70% (27,300) of them will arrive in a 45-minute period. You need to work out how many will arrive in three 15-minute periods. The trams can come every 3 minutes. If you divide the 15-minute number by 5, it will show how many people need to be transported every 3 minutes:

The maximum number of people the trams can carry is 500 every 3 minutes. Are there enough trams?

Check your thinking on page 31.

Time to start of event:	Percentage arriving:	Number arriving:	Every 3 minutes:
60–45 minutes	15%	4,095	
44–30 minutes	30%		
29–15 minutes	25%		

Research Note

• Trams
Excellent for: short city-centre journeys.
Three-car trams usually carry up to 250 people.

• Trains
Excellent for: longer or out-of-town travel.
Can carry large numbers of passengers; easy to add extra carriages.

THE FINAL DESIGN

Calculations show that it is impossible to carry enough people by tram. So in the final design, trams have been swapped with trains. Most of the time these will have just two or three carriages. On busy match-days, extra-long trains will be used.

Three-carriage platform

Passengers on these carriages can get off

Train moves forward to let more passengers off

REVISED DESIGN

MOVING PEOPLE TO AND FROM THE STADIUM

One of the biggest challenges for a stadium designer is nothing to do with designing the stadium itself. The challenge is, how do people get there and leave without it taking ages?

The user survey shows that over 70% of people think it is important to get this right. If a game is a sell-out, there will be 40,000 fans plus stadium workers. Are the transport links to the stadium good enough?

There are only 600 car-parking spaces. These are for staff, players and people with disabilities. Most people will travel either by bike or on a tram. In Northport, just over 2% of journeys are usually made by bike, so about 1,000 people will probably cycle. Roughly 39,000 will come by tram. The trams can run every 3 minutes, and each six-car tram can hold up to 500 people.

You need to work out if six-car trams every 3 minutes is enough!

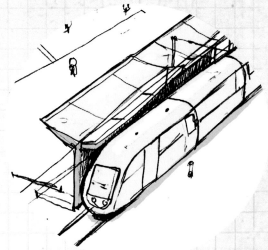

Tram stop large enough for a six-car tram

DREAM DESIGN

Research Note

Research shows that not all sports fans reach a stadium at the same time. The busiest time is between one hour and 15 minutes before the start. This is when 70% of fans arrive:

- 15% arrive 60–45 minutes before
- 30% arrive 44–30 minutes before
- 25% arrive 29–15 minutes before

Trams like this one in Dusseldorf, Germany are a great way to get around the city centre.

WORK IT OUT!

You need to decide whether any of the world's other stadiums suggest a solution to Northport's pitch problems. Look at the research note on page 14 and see whether any of the three stadiums there give you some ideas. You can check your thinking on page 31.

THE FINAL DESIGN

The final design is based on the Sapporo Dome, which has two playing surfaces. When grass is not needed, the pitch will be floated away to reveal the artificial turf underneath.

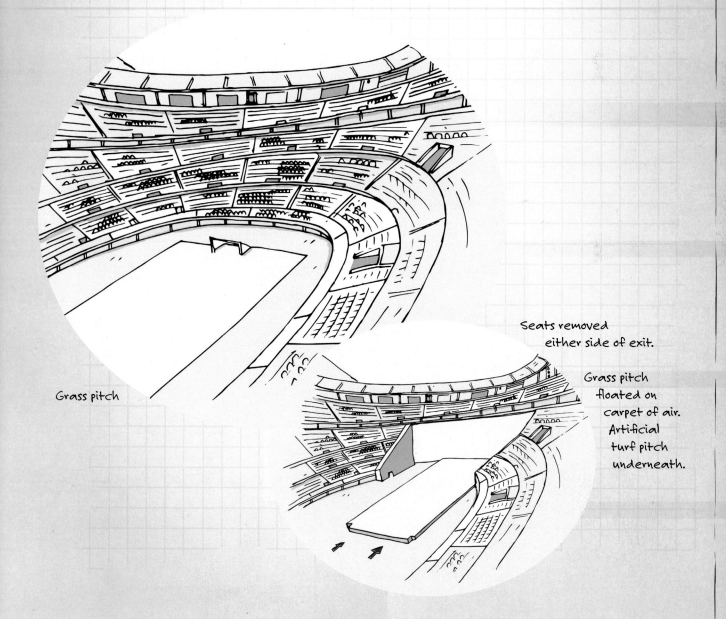

Grass pitch

Seats removed either side of exit.

Grass pitch floated on carpet of air. Artificial turf pitch underneath.

Research Note

Some of the world's busiest escalators are on the London Underground. There, people who want to be carried without walking stand on the right. The left side is free for people who want to go faster and walk. This is the fastest way to carry people along.

At least, that is what everyone thought.

In 2015, a test showed that an escalator could carry 81 people a minute if some people walked – but 113 people a minute if everyone stood still. The reason was that more people could fit on the escalator standing still.

'DO NOT WALK'

Research shows that when the escalators are going to be busy, a DO NOT WALK sign should be turned on. This will increase the number of people they can carry by 40%. But when should the computerised control system turn on the sign?

To know this, you need to work out how many people per minute the escalators can normally carry. If more people than this leave the station in one minute, it will be time to turn on the sign.

WORK IT OUT!

There are two up and two down escalators at each entrance. With the left side free for people who want to walk, each escalator can carry 63 people a minute.

Work out how many people in total the escalators can carry per minute. This will tell you when to turn on the DO NOT WALK sign.

Check your answers on page 31.

REVISED DESIGN

THE FINAL DESIGN

The final design is the same as the original design. (This does not usually happen!) There will be four entrances to the mall, each with two down escalators and two going up.

PROVIDE FOOD AND DRINK

The stadium's original design did not have anywhere for people to buy food or drink. The plan was for them to eat before they came in. They could use the restaurants and takeaway food services in the mall. But was this the right decision – and if not, what can be done about it?

DREAM DESIGN

ASK THE USER SURVEY

The user survey can help with this decision. A thousand people took part: 833 of them wanted to be able to buy tasty food and drink inside the stadium. In fact, it was one of the three most important things. It even came higher than having a comfortable seat.

So, the stadium needs to provide food and drink. But if you add lots of kitchens and restaurants to the design, they will only be used on match days. The rest of the time they would be empty – which is a waste.

What is needed is a way to keep people supplied with food and drink, without having to build lots of kitchens and food stalls.

Research Note

In Mumbai, India, hot food is delivered by dabbawallahs. The dabbawallahs collect hot meals from where they are cooked, and take them to a collection point. Then the meals are sorted according to destination, and transported across the city. Finally, another dabbawallah delivers the food.

Design a menu of food for the stadium. (This will be fun to do with two or three friends.)

There is no correct answer to the menu challenge, but your menu has to include:

- Four hot things to eat, one of them vegetarian
- Three cold things, one vegetarian
- Three different drinks

Try to include things most people like. And remember, everything on the menu has to be easy to eat while watching a football match. A bowl of hot soup might not be a great idea! A hot pie would be better.

THE FINAL DESIGN

The stadium is going to use a kind of dabbawallah system to get food to fans. Wearing yellow jackets will be people walking up and down collecting orders. These orders, plus a seat number, will be whizzed by computer down to a kitchen. A second team of people, wearing red jackets, will deliver the food from the kitchen to where it is wanted.

Stand: East 3
- - - - - - - - - - - - - - -
Tier: Red Seat: 594
- - - - - - - - - - - - - - -
Order:
- - - - - - - - - - - - - - -
Veggie burger, fries, strawberry milkshake
- - - - - - - - - - - - - - -
Northport Stadium

One kitchen will feed each side of the stadium.

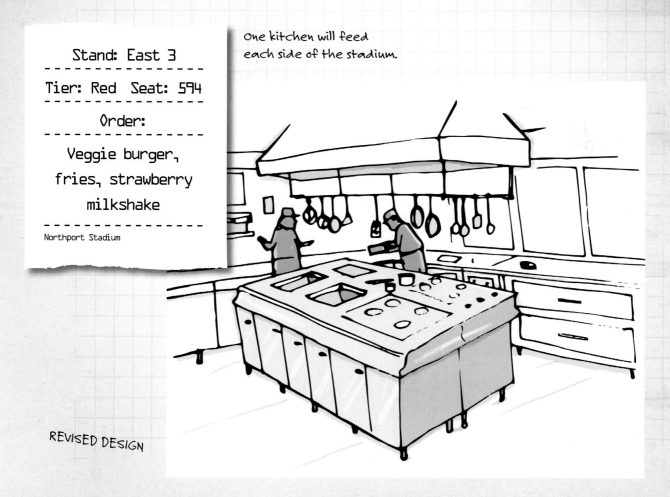

REVISED DESIGN

SEATING FOR EVERYONE

The dream design has some really dreamy seats! They are like the ones in Business Class on an airplane. They are wide and padded. The armrests even have a touchscreen inside. You can pull it out and rewind bits of the match, switch views and even give the referee a score.

ONE BIG PROBLEM

There is one big problem with the dream seats. They are really expensive. Business Class seats on an airplane cost over £20,000 each, and take up to 3 years to design. (First Class seats cost even more. Some have 2,000 separate parts and cost up to £340,000.)

£20,000 x 40,000 fans = £800,000,000.

Even a billionaire would think 800 million pounds was a lot of money for some seats. And as it is over twice the budget for the entire stadium, the seat cost will have to be cut. So the next job is to design seats that are comfortable, but much less expensive.

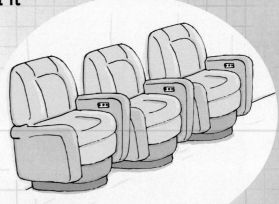

DREAM DESIGN

Business-class airline seat: typical width, 55cm.

Research Note

As well as ordinary seats, all stadiums in Europe have to make sure people with disabilities can come to events. There are rules about how many easy-access seats a stadium should have. In a stadium with 40,000 seats or more, there should be 210 (plus two more for every 1,000 above 40,000).

An organisation called Level Playing Field (www.levelplayingfield.org.uk) provides information about this for stadium designers and others.

WORK IT OUT!

Draw up an alternative seat design, including measurements for the width and depth. Remember:

1) People want seats that are wide, padded and comfortable.

2) Most stadium seats are about 43cm wide and between 41 and 44cm deep. (The seats at Wembley Stadium in London are unusually large. They are 50cm wide and 80cm deep.)

3) The seats have to flip up, so that people can move along the rows easily.

Start by doing an Internet image search for seat designs. A search for 'stadium seats' will bring up hundreds of images.

THE FINAL DESIGN

In the final design, the seats are as wide and deep as the ones at Wembley Stadium. They are also slightly padded. The padding makes them more expensive, but much more comfortable than most stadium seats. The seats cost £53.50 each, or £2,140,000 in total. This is a saving of £797,860,000 on the original design!

Economy airline seat
Width: 43cm

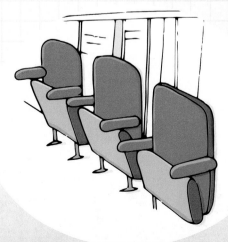

New design
Padding
Width: 50cm

Way wider
than an airline
economy seat!

REVISED DESIGN

PROVIDE THE STADIUM WITH POWER

A sports stadium needs a lot of power – especially one with a removable pitch and a sliding roof. It also needs power for floodlights during night-time matches. And like all big buildings, it will use power for things like lights, heating, cooling, computers and cleaning.

A busy sports stadium uses a lot of energy – and where that energy comes from has a big effect on the environment.

Retractable roof

Floodlights (inside roof)

Moveable pitch

Offices

DREAM DESIGN

POWER PROBLEMS

There are two problems with needing so much energy. First, it is expensive. Second, it may be bad for the environment. Most electricity in Britain comes from power stations that burn coal. Burning coal releases large amounts of carbon dioxide (CO_2) gas. This is one of the gases causing the rise in the Earth's temperature known as global warming.

   Part of the solution would be to use energy that does not come from coal-burning power stations. But is this possible?

Research Note

Renewable energy comes from sources that will not run out:

Solar power comes from the sun; more sunshine produces more energy.

Hydroelectricity is produced from moving water, such as rivers or tides.

Wind power is produced from wind; the turbines start to work at about 12kph.

Geothermal energy is produced using the heat within the Earth.

Biomass energy comes from the remains of living things that have died.

WORK IT OUT!

Look back at the research note about weather on page 12, and read the research note on page 24.

Are there any obvious forms of renewable energy that could be used at the stadium? Check your thinking on page 31.

Design inspiration! The stadium at Lincoln Financial Field in the USA uses wind turbines and solar cells to produce its own energy.

THE FINAL DESIGN

The final design will have two new energy-gathering features. First, some of the 'fish scales' on the sides of the stadium will be replaced with solar cells. These turn sunlight into electricity. They will power the stadium's offices and changing rooms.

The stadium will also have wind turbines along each of its long sides. The wind usually comes from the north-east, and the turbines will be able to catch its full power. They will be providing power day and night, all through the year.

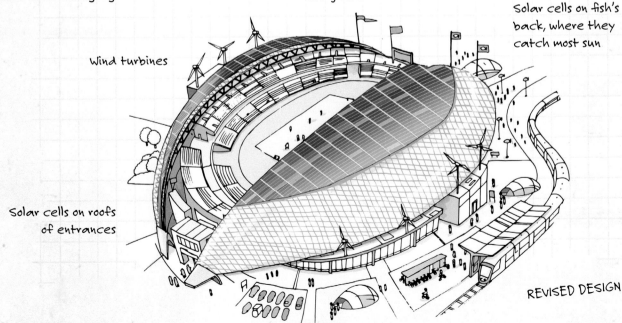

Wind turbines

Solar cells on roofs of entrances

Solar cells on fish's back, where they catch most sun

REVISED DESIGN

DESIGN A TEAM KIT

There is one design job still to do. The team needs a new kit, to go with their amazing new stadium. The design has to use Northport's city colours, which are blue and white. Apart from that, the kit can be anything you want (as long as Tracey Clacker likes it too!).

Northport's kit has not changed since the old black-and-white days.

KIT DESIGN, STEP 1

Designing a team kit is like designing anything else. The first step is to research the subject. Look at other teams' kits, as well as Northport's old one. Seeing the shapes and patterns that already exist will give you some ideas. It will also make sure that you do not accidentally copy someone else's design!

The new kit will use the city's colours, blue and white.

Research Note

Team strips from the 2014 World Cup:

Germany: kit is one main colour, with a single dash of another

Australia: simple design with shirts one colour and shorts another

Croatia: this checkerboard shirt is unlike any other team strip.

Mexico: blocks of colour plus a shape

Portugal: stripes blend two shades of colour together

Argentina: simple blue-and-white stripes. Stripes like this have always been a popular style.

KIT DESIGN, STEP 2

The best way to find colour combinations and shapes that work well together is to try them out. The next step is to start drawing out patterns and adding colours you think will look good. Some designers like to do this using pencils and paper, before transferring their designs to computer. Others use a computer from the beginning. There are tools on the Internet that can help you do this. (Search for 'online team strip design tool'.)

WORK IT OUT!

Come up with a choice of three team strips for the club's owner to pick from.

The templates will help you do this. Trace or copy them, scan them on to computer, or use an online team-strip design tool.

Your design will also need to include the logo of the owner's company on the chest:

In type big enough to go across the chest of the shirt above, filling about 1/3 of its width:

Tracey's Fab Fones

And on the back of each shirt will be the player's number and name:

THE FINAL DESIGN

The final design chosen is a pair of plain white shorts and a blue top. The top has a white collar and edge around the V-neck. Down each side is a blue-and-white checkerboard pattern.

THE BEST EVER SPORTS STADIUM?

Finally, the design is complete. Everything from how people are going to get there to where they will sit has been thought through. The food, drink, shopping, the power supply, pitch, roof – every big part of the design has been double checked. Finally, the plan for the world's best sports stadium is finished.

Wind turbines
These will harvest energy from the area's constant breezes.

Retractable roof acts like an umbrella
This will provide shelter, but still allow air to get inside.

Grass playing surface
Artificial playing surface
Having two surfaces means many sports can be played at the stadium.

Entrances on both sides

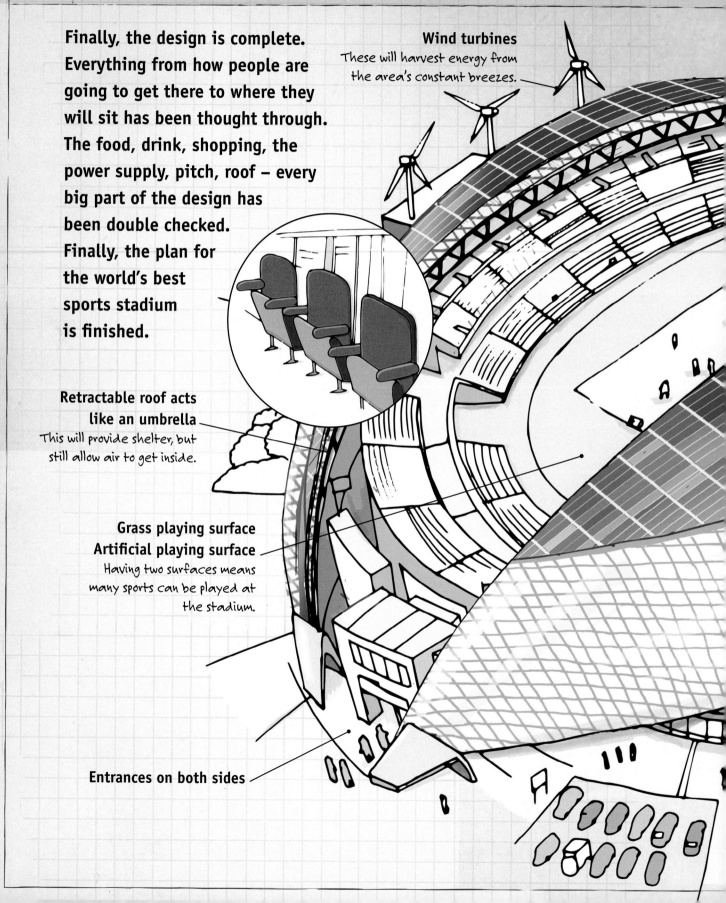

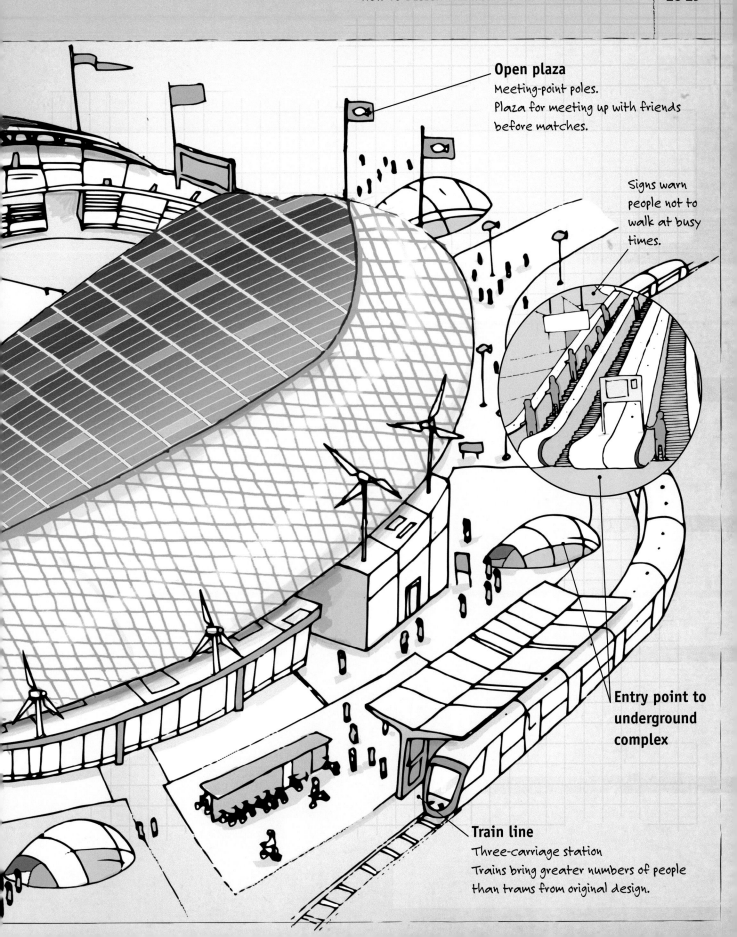

Open plaza
Meeting-point poles.
Plaza for meeting up with friends
before matches.

Signs warn
people not to
walk at busy
times.

**Entry point to
underground
complex**

Train line
Three-carriage station
Trains bring greater numbers of people
than trams from original design.

OTHER TOP SPORTS STADIUMS

The Silver Fish Stadium is a great design – but you cannot visit it, because it has not been built yet! If you want to see one of the world's actual top stadiums, here are some well known ones:

Allianz Arena
LOCATION: Munich, Germany
Opened: 2005
Nicknamed Schlauchboot, German for 'the inflatable boat', because of its bulbous design. Allianz Arena changes colour depending on which team is playing there.

National Aquatics Centre
LOCATION: Beijing, China
OPENED: 2008
Nicknamed 'the water cube'. The blue tiling effect outside matches the watery interior. Several copycat buildings have been built elsewhere in China.

Scotiabank Saddledome
LOCATION: Canada
OPENED: 1983
The stadium's saddle-back is a reminder of Calgary's cowboy history and culture (the city hosts a huge annual rodeo). There are no internal supports to spoil the fans' view.

National Stadium
LOCATION: Taiwan
OPENED: 2009
The first stadium in the world to be powered almost entirely by solar energy. The roof (which is shaped to make people think of dragons) is completely covered in solar panels.

Wembley Stadium
LOCATION: London, England
OPENED: 2007
One of the world's most famous football stadiums, Wembley's famous arch can be seen from all over London. Wembley is so big it could hold 7 billion pints of milk, or 25,000 double-decker buses.

Principality Stadium
LOCATION: Cardiff, Wales
OPENED: 1999
The Principality Stadium is famous for the intimidating noise of 74,500 Wales rugby roaring their team on. It is especially loud when the retractable roof is closed.

Germany's Schlauchboot, or 'inflatable boat', stadium is home to one of Europe's top football teams, Bayern Munich F.C.

'WORK IT OUT' ANSWERS

for p.10

55% of £350 million is

55 ÷ 100 x 350,000,000 = £192.5 million

35% of £350 million is

35 ÷ 100 x 350,000,000 = £122.5 million

10% of £350 million is

10 ÷ 100 x 350,000,000 = £35 million

To check your answer add together the three amounts: 192.5 + 122.5 + 35 = 350

for p.11

To work out the area of a rectangle you multiply its height by its width. The exposed tile will measure 0.9m x 0.9m (because 1m - 0.1m overlap = 0.9m). Each tile will have an area of $0.9 \times 0.9 = 0.81m^2$.

The side of the fish has an area of $30,788m^2$.

30,788 ÷ 0.81 = 38,010 tiles

38,010 x 2 = 76,020 titles in total.

for p.12

The calculation is 540 ÷ 1000 x 100 = 54%. So 54% of people prefer to be sheltered from bad weather. Of the rest, 38.7% like to be outdoors and 7.3% do not mind.

for p.13

A fabric roof like the one in Warsaw would not be a good idea. The stadium's local weather often has rain and temperatures below 5°C. Both of these would mean the roof could not be closed/opened.

A solid roof that works like an umbrella would be fine.

for p.15

Having two different playing surfaces, like at the Sapporo Dome, would be a great solution.

for p.17

Time to start of event:	Percentage arriving:	Number arriving:	Every 3 minutes:
60–45 minutes	15%	4,095	819
44–30 minutes	30%	8,190	1,638
29–15 minutes	25%	6,825	1,365

There are nothing like enough trams! A way of moving more people to the stadium is needed.

for p.19

2 x 63 = 126, so each entrance can move 126 people in one direction.

4 x 126 = 504, so in total the four entrances can move 504 people a minute.

The computer should be programmed to turn on the DO NOT WALK sign whenever 504 people leave the tram station within one minute of each other.

(To work out how many more people the escalators can carry with the sign on, you need to work out 140% of 504. This is: 140 ÷ 100 x 504 = 705.6.)

for p.25

The two obvious forms of renewable energy are:
1) Solar, because the stadium gets at least six hours of sunshine a day for most of the year;
2) Wind, because the average wind speed is always more than the speed needed for wind power.

GLOSSARY

architect designer of buildings

artificial turf pretend grass, which can be used as a playing surface for sports such as baseball, football and hockey

budget amount of money available

climate typical weather over a long period of time

easy-access seat seating that can be used by someone with a disability, particularly a wheelchair user

exposed visible or uncovered

global warming increase in the Earth's air and sea temperatures, which is causing damaging changes in the planet's weather

lease let someone use your property in return for regular payments

live as it happens

scales thin plates that protect the skin of fish and reptiles

search terms instructions given to an Internet search engine

solid not flexible or bendy

spectator person watching something happen

telecomms short for telecommunications (which are long-distance communications using the telephone network)

turbine spinning wheel a bit like a propellor, which gathers energy as it spins

user survey set of questions answered by users

INDEX

artificial turf 14, 15
athletes 4

budget 10, 22

car-parking spaces 16

dabbawallahs 20, 21

energy 24, 25, 30
entrances 8, 19, 28
environment 24
escalators 18, 19

floodlights 24
food and drink 4, 7, 20, 21, 28
football 6, 8, 14, 21, 30

Gehry, Frank 11
gymnastics 4

hockey 14

Internet 5, 11, 15, 23, 27

Olympics 4

people with disabilities 16, 22
playing surfaces 14, 15, 28
pitch 4, 7, 14, 15, 24, 28
power 24, 25, 28, 30

research 5, 6, 8, 12, 14, 16, 17, 19, 26
restaurants 8, 9, 20
roof 9, 12, 13, 24, 28, 30
rugby 14, 30

seats 4, 6, 7, 8, 12, 14, 20, 22, 23
shopping mall 6, 8, 9, 10, 18, 19, 20, 28, 29

solar cells 25
spectators 4
sports centre 8

team kit 26, 27
tiles 11
toilets 4, 7
trains 7, 17, 29
trams 9, 10, 16, 17, 29
transport 7, 16

weather 6, 7, 9, 12, 13, 25
wheelchair users 7
wind turbines 24, 25, 29

user survey 6, 7, 8, 10, 12, 16, 20

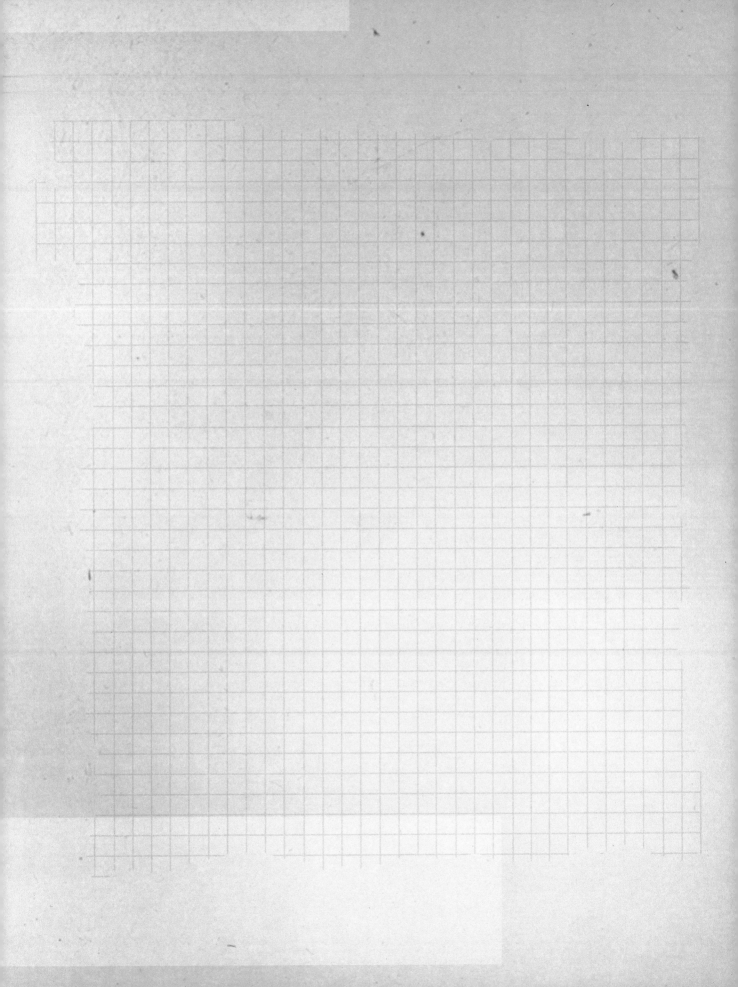